I'm Married
Now What

Understanding The Principles of Marriages

Tiatay Shiner

Published by Living Water Book, Christian Publishing House,

Little Rock, Arkansas 72201

Livingwaterbooks.org

Print Book Edition 2023

ISBN 979-8-9879261-1-6

Referenced: Gary Chapman- *The 5 Love Languages*

Living Water Books

John 7:38

He who believes in me, as the scripture has said,
Out of his heart will flow rivers of living water.

Dedication

This book is dedicated to my children Makayla, Tayvon, and Dj- thank you for being my inspiration and my driving force. Everything I do is because of you.

Acknowledgements

*To Victoria Belton, thank you for being
my mentor and helping me birth my vision.*

*To LaDeidre Maris of Living Water Books, thank you for your
patience and guidance. There were times when I was doubtful, but
you reassured me that God has a vision and a purpose for me. I
truly appreciate you.*

*To my pastors Robert and Katrina Wallace,
thank you for your spiritual counsel.*

*To my parents Cortez and Deborah, thank you for raising me to
the best of your ability. Thank you for instilling in me morals and
values that I carry throughout my life and pass on to my children.*

*To my husband Darrell, thank you for being my safe space. You
bring laughter and calmness to my sometimes too serious lifestyle.
I love you!!*

Table of Contents

Introduction

Congratulations! You did it! You tied the knot!

The ceremony is over, the guests are gone and now it's just you and your spouse. *So now, what?* If you're anything like I was, you have no clue what comes next.

- What does it mean to be married?

- What are you expected to do?

- Do you move into his place?

- Does he move into yours or do you get rid of them both and find something new?

- What about kids?

- Do you immediately get started having a family or do you wait a year or two?

- Are you expected to be a housewife, or will you try to manage both a career and family?

I am sure you have many questions about the journey you are about to embark on. Depending on who you ask, you will get different responses from different people. Each generation has their own expectations and ways of handling a marital situation. Lucky for you, I am here to give you some credible guidance. I'm going to share information that I didn't have when I became a newlywed. I'm going to share the lessons I've learned from my own experience of being married, plus tips I have picked up from books, podcasts, seminars, and regular conversations with married couples, both old and young.

My hopes are that this information will point you in the right direction to reduce any fears and or anxiety you may have regarding marriage. Prior to my marriage I didn't think that it would be possible for me to be wed. For the longest, I thought that I would never have two kids, a house, and a career. Marriage was never a thought of mine because I did not have a positive example of marriage, I could point to, growing up. My parents divorced when I was young, and my father married two more women and divorced them all before I was ten years old. So, naturally I thought I would be cursed in this area. Divorce and separation ran through my family on both sides. In addition, most of my friends were raised in a single parent household, with the exception of two friends but their parents were much older. So, a life of marriage didn't resonate with me.

My ideals of marriage came from television shows. These were my real-life examples, shows such as, *The Cosby Show, Family Matters* and *Roseanne* exhibited what I thought were good examples of healthy relationships. Those programs showed what it meant to be able to balance it all. In the marriage, they show loved and respect for one another and they also displayed how to handle conflict. They taught their children valuable lessons and I liked that. I knew if I ever got married, this would be my life road map.

If you haven't gotten married yet, and you are in the dating phase, have you prepared yourself for the concept of marriage? Do you know what it takes to be married? Have you spoken to any married couples, read books or listened to a podcast on marriage? Have you enrolled in premarital classes or counseling? Have you changed your mindset from "me" to "we"? Have you let go of past traumas and worked on yourself? These are some of the things that should be done, before getting married.

Part One

Building A Lasting Foundation

Section I

PREPARATION

Chapter One

Preparation

The preparation phase is the process of preparing oneself to be in a relationship with another. It involves taking a step back, looking deep down inside and figuring out what makes you, into you. It's asking yourself a series of thought-provoking questions that may bring up some hard feelings. Questions like, what things were you taught as a child or seen as a child that you now carry over into your relationships? How has this shaped how you see people of the opposite sex? What is your religion? How were you raised to view marriage through that religion? How does this knowledge of marriage affect your intended spouse that you choose? How would people describe you? What would you say are your strengths and weaknesses? What areas do you need to improve in? In your previous relationships, do you go after a certain type? Is this type good or bad? Is it giving you the desired outcome that you want?

Are you willing to walk away from this person to get the partner that you want? All these questions are important, which may cause your feelings and emotions to get fluffed, because the preparation stage requires transforming your mind!

Preparation is also a season for you to focus on yourself. It may also mean cutting ties with people from your past and making yourself available for only your future mate. You can't start something new if you have unfinished chapters in your life. Hanging on to old boyfriends/girlfriends only confuses things and slows down your progress.

I personally decided to do some self-reflection and soul searching before marriage. I had to heal from past traumas such as the abandonment issues I carried from my parents' divorce. My parents divorced when I was young, and my father gained custody of me and my sister. I went from seeing my mom every day to seeing her on the weekends and summer vacations. As I got older, the visits became few and far in between. This was hard for me because I wanted to be with her. I wanted us to have the same relationship as

I saw my friends have with their mothers. I didn't understand divorce, or how it worked. This was because no one was talking to me about it.

When I got older and started dating, I would ask my mom questions about how to handle certain situations. She always gave vague answers or referred me to my Bible. She would say "Pray about it." She came from a generation where you didn't discuss certain things, and you certainly didn't talk about them with a child. However, because of these unspoken truths in our relationship, I was confused and left to figure life out on my own. I believe this caused me to become a people pleaser and turned to other people for acceptance and validation. I wanted to belong to someone. I wasn't comfortable being alone, so I became a serial dater--trying to fill a void. I started jumping from one relationship to the next. Each relationship became worse than the previous one. I was not taking the time to look back and learn any lessons. I accepted and tolerated lies, cheating, and disrespect because I thought it was what I deserved. I no longer valued myself or required others to see the value in me.

I needed to change and regain focus. I had to relearn how to love myself. I had to look at the men I was dating and the reasons why I was choosing them. Honestly, I was basing my decisions on looks, which is a form of lust. I was being led by my flesh and not my spirit. I was young and naïve with no experience of what to seek in a mate. Everything I learned about selecting a mate, I learned from TV. He had to be tall, attractive, with nice hair and good teeth, have great taste in clothing and be financially stable. I was not selecting men based on character, morals, values, and standards.

In other words, I was choosing men based on their superficial exterior—that included their physique, money, and status. Once I changed and started looking at their core values, my dating pool started to change, and my experiences got better. I started looking for specific qualities, such as

- God fearing

- Good communicator

- Family oriented

- Kind and compassionate

- Hard working

- Honest, faithful, and loyal

- Responsible and trustworthy

- Respectful

In the beginning, before I had any experience, and had an innocence about myself, I saw only good in people. I wanted to be their friend and establish a nice, healthy, and whole foundation. I also required a title and commitment before having sex. I didn't have sex in the first six months of the relationship. I set boundaries and I was serious about holding my partner accountable. If they told me we were going on a date on a certain day, at a certain time, I held them to that. If they said they were going to call at a certain time, and they didn't, I held them to that. When those relationships didn't work out, I felt like I had been burned so I would use my sexuality to maintain the relationship. I felt like that's what men wanted and that's what they needed, so that is what I would give them. On the outside, my clothes and appearance were conservative, but my mind and body were hypersexual. My conservation was always about sex, so of course guys saw me as nothing more than someone to have sex with. Nothing I presented said that I wanted to settle down, be married, and have kids. I came to the realization that I had to change all of that if I wanted to attract better men in my life.

I had a very strong personality, which meant I was controlling, bossy and direct. This behavior was very intimidating to men and needed my immediate attention. I knew if I wanted a partner and subsequent marriage, I would have to make room for someone to come into my life and lead. Everything couldn't be my way. This was hard for me to adjust to because I was raised to be independent. However, if I'm doing everything or have an "*I don't need you*" attitude, it will make the other person have feelings that they are unwanted, not needed, and undervalued. Relationships are about give and take. It is a dance between two people. Both people can't lead. Someone must be willing to follow. Preparation teaches us to see through the lens that covers our eyes, then seek God regarding healing, so that our eyesight changes. Self-discovery is so important and rewarding, if we first allow God to examine our hearts and show us a mirror of ourselves.

PRINCIPLES FOR SELF-DISCOVERY

- Take a step back and create a new normal of being alone.

- Use this time alone to reflect on past relationships.

- Focus on self-care and the things you love.

- If you desire to be married, you must think marriage.

- Cut all ties and communications with your previous partners.

Chapter Two

The Meeting

It was a hot, sunny day in the summer of 2007, and I had gone to my apartment complex laundromat. I was at the front office loading money on my card when he walked in behind me. I was having issues with the card when he said, "Hurry up." I turned around with an attitude prepared, to go off. When I turned around, he was standing there in a light blue velour jogging suit, with no shirt underneath, white tennis shoes, and a hat turned backward. He had the biggest smile on his face.

When I looked down, he had the most adorable little girl with him. She looked like she was between the ages of one or two years old. I quickly refrained myself and told him I was having trouble with the card. He introduced himself, and said his name was Luke. He took the card from me and walked towards the machine. Somehow, he was able to figure it out and get the card loaded. I said, "Thank you!"

and proceeded to walk away. A few moments later, we were together again in the laundromat. Luke asked how long I had been living in the apartment complex. I told him that me and my best friend were new to the apartment complex. We engaged in a casual conversation that lasted probably an hour. Towards the end of the conversation, we exchanged numbers.

When I got to my car, I called my best friend. I told her that I had met a really nice guy, there was only one problem, he was missing his front teeth. She said, "What?" She burst out laughing and was like, "Tia, no!" I said, "Yes and he has a kid." Then she really said, "No!" I had been known to pick the wrong men. I had spent the last seven years in one failed relationship after the next. I was finally at a place in my life where I was focusing on just myself and I was doing well in my career.

My best friend and I had just got our new place and things were beginning to look up for me. A new relationship was the last thing on my mind. A few weeks went by, Luke called and asked if I would like to go out on a date. I was hesitant, but I said, "Yes." I wasn't ready for a solo date so I asked if my friend could come along and we could go bowling. Luke agreed and brought his friend James along. We had a good time at the bowling alley. We had a chance to talk a little, but we kept it light.

Afterwards, we went back to his house to chill. Just so happen, I already knew his friend because we use to work together. James told me that Luke was a good dude and they had known each other for a while. James was a good judge of character, so I trusted him. I had no reason to believe he would steer me in the wrong direction. It started getting late and I had to work the following morning. Luke walked me to my car and said, "I would like to see you again but next time alone." I agreed and we made plans to go out to dinner.

The plans were finalized and we met for dinner there we talked about our upbringing and things from our past. We had a lot of things in common. Luke told me that he was recently divorced and had two small children. When I asked why they divorced, he said religious reasons and infidelity issues ended their marriage. Luke said he was in the process of starting over. After dinner, he drove me home and we sat in the car talking. He told me that he had a really nice time, and he enjoyed my company. Luke made me laugh. I smiled a lot when I was with him, and I liked that. Over time, we continued to talk and build a friendship.

Luke was an attractive guy and had the body of a gymnast. His abs were amazing, skin was smooth, and he was well groomed. I tried hard not to make the friendship about sex. I wanted this relationship to be different from my past experiences. I made sure I didn't put myself in situations that could lead to sex. We had been talking for a few months when Luke invited me to attend his company gala. I was both surprised and impressed. This was my first time dating someone who had a professional career.

The gala required us to wear formal attire. Luke took me to the mall and bought me a gown. The gown was beautiful. It was satin, two tone, black on one side and white on the other. He had to wear a tuxedo. I liked the fact that he was introducing me to something new that I had never experienced. At the gala, Luke introduced me to all his co-workers and boss as his girlfriend. I was surprised because we had never really had that conversation, but I was happy, none the less that he was thinking of me in that manner. The night went on and we had a great time. Luke took me home and I learned about his multiple layers, that he could be professional during the day and laid back and chill at night. The next important date following the gala, was when I told Luke I that I would come to his home and make him dinner. He lived alone, so we would have more privacy. Up until this point we hadn't had sex. It had been close to six months and I arrived at his apartment with groceries in hand. He let me in and showed me to the kitchen. Luke told me he needed to take a shower because he had just come home from the gym. I said, okay and started dinner. Halfway through making the dinner, he emerged in the kitchen with a robe on. It was opened at the top, so his chest and abs were exposed. I knew he was trying to tempt me, and it was working. I said, "You think you slick!" He replied, "What did I do?" We ate dinner and talked but I was distracted. I could no longer fight back the urge to sleep with him. I had held back long enough. I walked over to him and straddled across his lap. I began kissing him

24

passionately. He stood up and scooped me up and carried me into the bedroom. He already had music and candles going but that was just his vibe. I quickly undressed and he got undressed. He put the condom on, and well I can only describe it as a sexual explosion. We literally had sex for hours. It was like nothing I had ever experienced before. He was aggressive and dominant but in a good way. He knew what he wanted and what pleased him. He was sure of himself and his abilities.

After that encounter, we became inseparable. We had different work schedules, but we would make time for each other. If I had to work the night shift, Luke would meet me during his lunch break. He even gave me a key to his apartment, which made it official. Handing me that key to his apartment meant that he wasn't seeing anyone else. He trusted me enough to have access to his space. He wanted me in his life. He wanted a future with me in it. We began to spend more time together. I was at his place more than I was at my own. Despite all the time that we were spending together and all the sex we were having, I knew that I had an end goal in mind. I wanted to be married, have kids, and buy a house. He had already done those things and I wasn't sure if he wanted to travel down that road again. I built up the courage and I told him what I wanted. He said he was fine with that. By the beginning of the following year, we were planning to start a family.

We all know the childhood song, *first comes love, then comes marriage, then comes the baby carriage*. Unfortunately, things didn't happen for me in that order. I had my concerns about having a baby. Two years prior, I had been diagnosed with endometriosis, which is a disorder in which the uterine tissues that normally lines the uterus grows outside the uterus. It causes painful periods and pain with intercourse. It can result in infertility. I had a laparoscopy done to remove the scar tissue to increase my chances of getting pregnant. Now I had to see if it would work. I was also concerned about miscarrying since that had happened to me before.

Once we made the decision to try for a baby, it didn't take long before I became pregnant. We both were so happy. I was happy because this baby was planned and was made from love. We both were financially secure and had housing. This situation was a lot different from my previous pregnancy experiences. Luke came to every doctor's appointment. He was there to help me with my morning sickness, which lasted the entire pregnancy. He was attentive and catered to my needs. Luke made the process smooth and relaxing. I couldn't have asked for a better partner.

PRINCIPLES FOR MEETING YOUR MATE

- Find someone that you feel comfortable being around and allows you to be yourself.

- Find someone that possess core values – honesty, integrity, respect for self and others, and who is hardworking.

- Find someone that has proven they are capable of being on their own, that way they are not dependent upon you and they can take care of you, if something was to happen

Section II

PARTNERSHIP

Chapter Three

The Wedding

As I mentioned earlier, we did things out of the traditional order.

Tradition says first comes love, then comes marriage, then come the

baby and baby carriage. Well, we had a baby first, bought a house

and then got married. At the time of the marriage, neither one of us

was involved in the church. We both had religious backgrounds and

upbringings, but for whatever reason, we didn't attend. Luke said he

didn't go to church because he had a bad experience with the pastors.

To him, they were known for taking money from the church and not

helping the church members. For me, my challenge was being

forced to attend church as a child. While visiting my mom on the

weekends, we would go to church. She would dress me up in an

itchy lace dress and white stockings. We would be in church for

hours, sometimes we would attend multiple services. I could never say I didn't want to go, I had to go! When I got old enough, I made the decision for myself, I decided I didn't need to attend church.

For those reasons, we decided that we could have the wedding in the backyard of our new home. I looked into other venues, but they were either too expensive or too big for the size wedding that we were having. We picked the colors crimson red and white. We ordered the decorations and the flowers. I did most of the planning and work. Since he had been married before, he wasn't as excited or involved as I would have liked him to be. This hurt me a little because I wanted him to have the same excitement for our wedding as he did for his first wedding. Looking forward, I now know to advise my children to find someone who hasn't been married before and doesn't have any children, so they can experience those first together.

When the wedding day arrived, everything was beautiful. All of our friends and family were there. The girls were gorgeous in their flower girl dresses. The only downfall was we had the wedding in the late spring, beginning of summer at 2:00pm. The sun was beaming over the backyard. It was hot! During my excitement of planning, I didn't think about renting a tent! We were sweating in our dresses and suits. Guests tried their best to stay and have fun, but the sun and heat was getting the best of folks. Despite being uncomfortable, we had a good time. The food was delicious. We had catered BBQ with baked beans, green beans, spaghetti, and potato salad. Again, this wasn't your traditional wedding. The ceremony and reception lasted a few hours before we called it quits. We honeymooned at the Renaissance Hotel.

When we arrived at the hotel, the room was beautiful. It was a suite that overlooked the city. I picked out some sexy lingerie because I wanted the night to be special and romantic. Honestly, I don't remember much happening once we arrived. I think we both were too tired and exhausted from all the activities of the day. Now it wasn't like this would be our first time together so it felt good to rest. We were just happy to be married and to have all the planning behind us. Now we were moving forward as husband and wife.

PRINCIPLES FOR OVERCOMING TRADITIONAL AND PERSONAL CHOICES IN MARRIAGE

- Create a budget and stick to the budget. Don't try to keep up with the Joneses and enter the marriage in debt.

- Try to incorporate both partners' religion and interests.

- Do what works for you and your household!

- Be willing to comprise. You may not be able to get everything you want, but you can get something close to it.

- Have fun. Remember this is a joyful time. Do not let stress overtake you.

Chapter Four

Expectations

In most marriages, before tying the knot you meet with a pastor and undergo pre-marital counseling. Pre-marital counseling is an opportunity to sit down with your partner to discuss future topics and issues that may arise and how you plan to handle them. The most basic topics are finances, children, sex, conflict, and expectations. Expectations are based on your personal upbringing, religious and social culture. These experiences influence how you will behave and what you will expect. Neither one of us belonged to a church so we skipped this part. We did, however, have a conversation about our expectations.

We agreed that we would be faithful and honest to each other. We also agreed that we would maintain open, direct communication, and discuss matters that came up in our marriage. We agreed that we would not go to bed angry or with unresolved issues. If one of us needed a day to cool off, we would say that up front. I told him that I wasn't a fan of passive aggressive energy so I wouldn't tolerate the silent treatment. He told me that he didn't like it when I would leave the house after an argument. Neither one of us was allowed to disappear or leave the house for an extended period. We agreed not to argue in front of the children and most importantly, that all disagreements would be managed in a mature, respectful manner, with no name calling, yelling or profanity.

Regarding our finances, we decided that we would have a joint checking account. Both our checks would be deposited into one account. The account would be used for household bills. We could make small purchases from the account but large purchases over a certain dollar amount had to be discussed between us. We each were allowed to have a separate savings account. We could do what we wanted with those.

For the household work and chores, we took more of a traditional approach. I handled everything in the inside and Luke took care of the outside. In the wintertime, when it was less to do outside, he would help more around the house. He was adamant that he would not clean the bathrooms or wash clothes. I was okay with that. He also took the lead in maintaining the cars. He was responsible for oil changes, routine maintenance and washing the cars.

When it came to outside friends, we agreed about friends of the opposite sex. For me, I felt like it was too tempting. Yes, you can draw boundaries but not everyone will be respectful of those boundaries. In those situations, you must use judgement and discernment. If someone gives off the slightest hint that they don't respect your marriage, cut them off. Don't take any chances because It's not worth the risk. By simply eliminating the problem before it starts made sense for us. The same thing with social media. I never was a fan of social media. I felt like it was the devil. It's a breeding ground for temptation.

No two households are the same. What may work for one, may not work for the other. It is important to have conversations with your spouse to discuss plans on how different issues that may arise will be handled.

PRINCIPLES FOR EXPECTATION

- Communicate unrealistic expectations.

- Set goals for your marriage.

- Remember that you are two different people who are learning to become one.

- Do not expect your spouse to be you. Marriage doesn't need another you.

- Keep your marriage goals hidden in Christ.

Chapter Five

Finances

Now let us back up just a bit because in order to discuss the finances I have to go back prior to the marriage. As we were preparing for the baby, we thought it would be best if I moved out of the apartment with my best friend and move in with him. It did not make sense for me to pay the extra rent if I could live with him. The lease was ending soon, so I wasn't leaving her in a financial bind. We also decided to downsize his apartment. Luke currently had a two-bedroom, two-bathroom apartment. The extra room was used for his daughters, but they never used the room. This allowed us to save more money. Instead of putting my furniture in a storage, we stored it in his living room. No one came to visit us anyway, so it didn't bother us. As far as bills went, I paid the utilities, and he paid the rent. His car was paid for, and I still had a few more payments on mine, plus I still had to make the payments on my ex-boyfriend's car. We knew that we eventually wanted to buy a house, so we pulled our credit reports to see where we stood. I had a few medical bills but nothing major. For the most part, I stayed on top of my bills. I keep my credit cards low, and I made my payments regularly, on time. Luke's credit wasn't in bad shape, but it needed attention. The biggest thing was his child support order from his divorce. He didn't owe a huge balance, but because it was arrears, it was considered a collection. This looked negative on his report.

To improve his credit score, I added him as an authorized user to my credit cards, so when I made my payments, he would also receive credit towards his score. He did not have a physical card. We kept our accounts separate but once we got married, we did join accounts. He was skeptical at first. He said that he had done that with his previous wife, and she had overdrawn the account multiple times. I would be in control of the account, so he didn't have to worry about that. We both maintained separate savings accounts. Whenever we got extra money, we would put it towards his child support. He worked extra side jobs, and I got bonuses. We worked together toward the goal of paying a portion from each check and eventually we paid it off. Next, we tackled our finances by establishing a household budget that included rent, utilities, insurance, cell phones, gas, groceries, and miscellaneous items. We also set aside money for entertainment and travel.

By the time the summer ended, we were ready to buy the house. Luke found a realtor. She was knowledgeable and nice. She helped us to find a home in a good neighborhood that was within our budget. Although he had proved himself to be dependable and reliable, I didn't veer away from my rule; *I must be able to afford this on my own.* This was my motto for any financial situation that I put myself in. It kept me protected. God forbid that something bad would happen like such as we separated, or he lost his job. I wanted to be able to afford things on my own. I learned my lesson with my ex-boyfriend and the car that I co-signed for.

When it came down to financing the house, Luke's credit still hadn't gotten to where it needed to be. It wasn't the child support this time;

it was the student loans. He had defaulted on his payments. We didn't know how to fix that. Because I had the better credit everything had to go in my name, also because we weren't married at the time, he could not be on the loan. I didn't know that. I'm not sure if he did or not. I wasn't worried or skeptical because we had been together for a year by now, he hadn't missed any payments or quit his job. He was able to be added to the deed of the house. This served as a type of insurance for him. It basically gave him rights to the house if something was to happen to me.

In addition to financing, we secured down payment assistance through a first-time home buyer program. President Barack Obama had passed a bill that assisted families with the purchase of their first home. That year, when we filled out taxes, we made out like a fat rat! We had credit for the birth of our daughter and the purchase of a new home. We put half the refund in a savings account and spent the rest on our home. After we bought the house, we were still flying high. We enjoyed each other's company. We were able to sit back and look at what we had been able to accomplish in less than a year.

It was nice having a partner that was mature and stable. We didn't argue or have trust issues. I didn't have any problems with his children's mother. Everything was cool.

PRINCIPLES FOR FINANCES IN MARRIAGE

When it comes to finances, the goal is to do whatever is necessary for the betterment of the household. It requires teamwork. If one person is good with finances and the other is not, this is an opportunity to teach them what you know. The marriage can't be as successful if only one person is succeeding. If one person is a saver while the other person is a spender, this is counterproductive because you have to work twice as hard to accomplish your goals. The household finances are not a place for competition. It doesn't matter who makes the most money. The goal is to build and achieve together. Prior to getting married, it is recommended to have a conversation about finances.

You can start by asking the following questions:

1. What are your thoughts about money?

2. Do you pay bills on time or wait until the disconnection notice?

3. Do you pay bills in full or what you can afford?

4. Do you have a lot of debt? What type of debt do you have? (Student loans, car loans, credit cards, pay day loans,)

5. Have you had any repossessions, bankruptcies, or collections?

6. Do you know your credit score?

7. Are you a spender or a saver?

8. Do you have any life insurance?

Section III

PARENTING

Chapter Six

Child-Rearing

Luke was good with his children, I had never seen anything like it. They were the center of his world. He never missed a weekend picking them up. Even though they were young, ages one and two, he was attentive to their needs. They were his little princesses. His love for them reminded me of the relationship with me and my dad. I think that's why I gravitated towards him. Luke was caring and nurturing with those girls. He made their breakfast, changed their diapers, and gave them baths. He was a natural. He said it was because he had younger siblings that he helped raise. Me, I didn't know the first thing about childcare.

I am a middle child. I have an older sister and a younger brother. My sister is six years older than me, and my brother is 11 years younger than me. We were never raised in the same house and by the time I was 10, my older sister moved out to live with my mom. My younger brother came during my mother's second marriage. When I would visit my mother on the weekends, she didn't allow me to change his diapers or fix his bottles; she or my stepdad handled that. So, I had no experience caring for a child. Luckily, being with Luke helped prepare me for our first child.

Our daughter was born on December 27, 2008. She was 6 lbs. and 9 ounces and was a tiny little thing. She came out bright yellow, with a cone shaped head. I was afraid that her head was going to stay that way, but it eventually went down. My sister and my husband were in the delivery room with me. The next day, all our friends and family came to see her. She was special. She was my miracle baby.

When we arrived home, Luke did his best to take care of us. He was attentive to my needs and hers. I would wake up with her and do the nightly feedings while I was on maternity leave. I wanted him to get his rest. He was still working. I didn't want him to be tired. When it was time for me to return to work, we took turns caring for her however, he did it more than me. I started to feel bad for him. Everything was starting to take a toll on him. He was getting dark

47

circles around his eyes from lack of sleep. His gymnast body was starting to turn into a dad bod, but he never complained. He did what he had to do, even on the weekends when he had all the girls. I would work ten hours and when I came home from work; he would have all three of the girls lined up on the couch or on a blanket on the floor. They weren't crying at all.

In past generations, the man was the provider, and the woman was the homemaker. It was her responsibility to maintain the house, care for the children and take care of the man. It was the man's responsibility to earn the paycheck and provide for the family. The roles never switched or crossed. Since men spent so much time out of the house, they didn't have the opportunity to build bonds with their wives or children. Men didn't assist with bathing the children, checking homework and spending leisure time with the family. As time went on, and more women entered the work force, women became providers, just as well as the men. However, in many instances, in addition to working and earning money, women were still required to care for the home. That was me, I am her.

I worked 50-60 hours per week; days, nights, and holidays. It was my job to get myself ready and my daughter ready for daycare. I would feed her, pack her bag, and then drop her off before heading to work. My husband would pick her up in the evenings. We did a good job of balancing the load and sharing the responsibilities. Although, at times, he did carry more of the burden. We both disciplined our daughter. I didn't leave it up to him to be the only parent to discipline her because he said he didn't want to be the bad guy. I let him discipline his daughters.

Times have changed. Both men and women work outside of the home. The financial burden is often split between two people. With that being said, marriage requires both individuals to come together and share responsibilities for the upkeep of the home and the care of the children. No one person's job is more important than the other. If your job requires long hours and you are not able to contribute in other ways except in finances, have a conversation with your partner about what you are facing and the expectations. Maybe you cannot physically contribute to the household, but you can afford to get a nanny or a housekeeper. Having something in place to lighten the load, will reduce stress and free up time for you and your spouse. Again, every relationship and household are different. You must do what is best for you and your situation.

Child rearing is more than just providing the basics for them, food, clothes, and shelter. It also involves nurturing their emotional well-being. It is important to provide discipline but also a supportive structure. Children learn structure from you and your partner setting expectations. This lets them know what is expected of them and what the consequences will be if they don't follow your instructions. Structure is another form of love. It lets them know that you care about their well-being, and you want them to feel safe and secure. You want the best for them. You never want to see them hurt. You must show them by example how to be kind to themselves and others. You do this by teaching morals, values, and standards.

PRINCIPLES FOR RAISING CHILDREN

When you get married, it is important to have a conversation with your spouse about children and child- rearing.

1. Do you plan to have children?

2. How many do you want to have?

3. When do you plan to start having them?

4. Will someone stay home to raise them?

5. Do you prefer daycare?

6. How will they be raised?

7. What religion will they practice?

8. Are they going to play sports?

9. How do you plan to discipline the children?

10. Will this be a shared responsibility, or will one person be in charge?

Chapter Seven

Sex and Intimacy

Before we had our daughter, sex was not a problem. We were young and spontaneous. We would have sex all day, multiple times throughout the day. We would challenge each other to do things outside of the norm. If we were driving down the street at night, we would pull over and have sex in the car. Once, we had sex in the backseat of the car in his mother's driveway. We were young and wild. We longed for each other and wanted to make the other person happy.

When the baby came, things slowed down. Our priority switched from focusing on our needs to her needs. Now instead of being spontaneous, our sex life had to be planned out. We would have to wait until she went to sleep and work it around her schedule. We had three kids under the age of three. It was exhausting, plus our work schedules were demanding. I felt like I never had enough energy. This also made it harder to be intimate. It was hard and it did put a strain on our relationship. In addition to that, I started taking birth control pills. I did not want any more kids at the time but that didn't mean I wouldn't want them later. I had taken the birth control shot before but that caused me to gain a lot of weight. I thought the pills would be the better option for us but the longer I stayed on them, the more my body started changing.

I went from wanting sex all the time, to wanting it hardly ever. I really had to talk myself into the moment, and this was hard for us. It was hard for me because I was still very much attracted to my husband. Luke was sexy. I knew he was a great catch, and I knew other women would fine him desirable. I didn't want him to be tempted to cheat. It was hard for him because he didn't know what to do with his sexual frustration. Luke still desired me, but he felt like I was rejecting him or not caring about his needs. We talked about it, and I tried my best to meet his sexual expectations, but it wasn't enough. We went through a dry spell. Eventually, we figured out it was the birth control pills. I stopped taking them and soon my sex drive came back.

Intimacy is more than just the physical act of sex. It is the emotional and intellectual connection that you create with your spouse. You can show intimacy through in depth, meaningful conversations. You can express love through small acts of kindness like holding hands, gentle kisses, and playful banter. You can create intimate moments together spending quality time with one another; watching a movie, cooking a meal, and sharing ice cream.

In marriage, as your life evolves, your sex drive will change. There are things such as your jobs, children, health, and stress, which will impact on your sexual desire and cause a change. Sex may eventually feel routine and mundane. It's a part of life. It comes with the territory. The best thing to do is learn how to adapt quickly. Be open to learning new skills and trying new things, all within your comfort zone. You can invest in books, sex toys or find a sex therapist to talk about your challenges, fantasies or what turns you on. What may have worked a few months or years ago, may not have the same effect now. Don't let the dry spells between you and your spouse be the end of your marriage. Communication is key during this time. Express your needs and concerns and most importantly, be patient while you are waiting for answers.

PRINCIPLES FOR SEXUAL DESIRES

- Communicate about sexual needs and expectations.
- Make time for one another.
- Have fun and be adventurous to avoid boredom and sex becoming mundane.
- Find other ways to connect outside of the bedroom.

SECTION IV

PRIORITIES

Chapter Eight

Friends/Family

When you get married, the two of you become one. Everything you have as individuals should come together. This includes your family. Family members can serve as a support system, offering advice and assistance. However, there needs to be boundaries set in place. As you start to build your own immediate family, you will have less time for extended family. This may be an adjustment period, not everyone will be open and receptive to this phase. Some family members may become jealous and envious, so try not to take it personally. Just have a conversation with that family member and explain that your priorities have changed, you would love to spend time with them but not as much as you once did. You must establish a balance! Marriage is a covenant between you, your spouse and God. With that being said, keep family out of your relationship. Yes, there may be one or two members that you feel comfortable confiding in, but don't let everyone know what is going on in your relationship and household. This opens you up to unsolicited advice, criticism, and judgement. You don't need the opinions of five different people in your head; it just causes confusion. Not only that, once you move past the issue, your family may hold a grudge or harbor feelings towards your spouse. You don't need that.

Friendships have to be handled with boundaries as well. Especially, if they are single. Single people live a different lifestyle and operate by a different code. They do not have the same attachments and responsibility that you have. Most can stay out late partying, clubbing and bar hoping. They can talk to and entertain multiple people while blowing their money at the casinos, bars, and clubs. They can take trips whenever with whomever but you cannot. Your decisions affect someone else now. It is not just about you anymore. You must ask yourself; how would my spouse feel about this decision? How would I feel if my spouse did this same thing? The same rules apply to loaning money to family members. We love our families and always want to help when we can, but a conversation should be made before giving out money. If it's a few dollars that's not going to break the bank, that may be okay but again, it depends on the household. For substantial amounts that are equivalent to paying a bill or living expense, talk to your spouse first. Give them the respect of having an opinion or input towards the matter. This can be applied to caring for a loved one or allowing a loved one to stay with you.

Before you allow a loved one to come and stay with you, you and your partner should have a conversation to see how each person feels about the decision. How long is this person planning to stay? What will they be expected to do as far as contributing to the household? Are they expected to pay rent? Will they require transportation services or assistance with daily activities? Will there be other people joining them? All these questions are important to ask your spouse, because opening your home to another can put a strain on your relationship. You will lose your privacy and incur additional costs. ***Stay in constant communication.*** Be sure to let the other person know if your feelings about the situation have changed.

Chapter Nine

Blending A Family

I know in previous chapters I have two other beautiful girls so this chapter will give more insight regarding them because we need to discuss blended families! When I met Luke, he already had two small girls. I had only been in one other relationship with a person who had a child. My approach to this was to move slowly and build a relationship with the children first. I didn't want to come off trying to establish dominance or assert authority. Since the girls were so young, it was easier for me to develop a friendship. I took an interest in the things that mattered to them. My goal was not to appear as a replacement of their mom, but an extension. I wanted to be someone they could trust and feel comfortable talking to and being around. I wanted them to feel safe. I did not discipline them. I left that to their dad. However, he did have a talk with them to let them know that what I said mattered and they also had to follow my rules as well. I think it is important for the girls to see us in a living relationship. If they could see that I cared for their dad and I wouldn't hurt him, then they knew I would love and protect them as well. I also tried to establish a relationship with their mother. I invited her to our home and allowed her the chance to look around. I wanted her to be comfortable with knowing where her children would be spending time and the type of environment, they would be in. I allowed her to ask me whatever questions she needed to, to be comfortable with me being around her children. She wasn't receptive of my efforts, but that was her issue, not mine. I extended the olive branch and left the door open if she changed her mind. I think it is essential to establish boundaries with the ex- husband/wife or baby mama/daddy. That relationship is over, hallelujah and there should be no conversation outside of dealing with the children, however, this requires trust. If you have established a good relationship between all parents involved, maybe you can get to the point where phone numbers are exchanged. The goal is to do what is best for the children.

PRINCIPLES FOR BLENDED FAMILIES

I recommend not talking down about the other parent in front of the children. At some point this was someone that you cared for and shared a relationship with. For whatever reason it didn't work out but now you share a child together. The child is innocent. The child should not be subjected to arguments or abuse simply because the two of you have differences. If the child is age appropriate, maybe you can have a conservation with them about the relationship between you and that other parent. Children have questions and it's better to hear it from you as opposed to not having any answers at all.

Chapter Ten

Balancing Work and Life

Luke was a program manager. He worked Monday thru Friday from 9-5, no weekends or holidays, and he had a set schedule with more time off than I did. I, on the other hand was a retail store manager. I worked 50-60 hours per week, nights, weekends, and holidays. I earned vacation leave and sick leave, which I rarely used. Since I didn't have a set schedule, I felt like I was always on the go, especially on the days when I would close the store the night before and would have to be back to work the next morning. I felt like I never had time for my family. I missed them dearly when I was away from them. I would call my husband during my breaks and lunches just to stay connected and let him know that I was thinking of him. On my off days, I would keep my daughter home from daycare. I would take her to the park or zoo. I wanted to make sure that we had that bonding time, and either way, she still became a daddy's girl. For my husband, I would try to plan date nights and romantic evenings. I would cook his favorite meal or bring home his favorite snack. I knew that dealing with my schedule was hard, and I didn't want him to feel neglected. I would plan family vacations or weekend getaways for us. He did the same for me. He would cook dinner and try to time it so that it would be hot when I arrived home. He would buy me small gifts to say he was thinking of me. He would leave me cards and thoughtful notes in my car, for me to read on my way to work. On the weekends, he would bring the girls to my job to have lunch with me. On my off days, I would go to his job and have lunch with him.

Outside of each other, we had our own interests and hobbies. I liked to spend time with my friends and family. I would visit them and just sit around and talk. I would also meet up with them and have lunch or dinner. It wasn't very often. I didn't get many off days so when I did, I wanted to be with my family. Luke was into restoring old cars, training dogs, and doing work outs at the gym. That was his way of decompressing and getting a break from married life. It is important to have your own hobbies and interests, which gives you time away from each other to recharge and miss the other person. That can't happen if you are always together. You won't have anything to talk about because you are always together. I have included some lessons on love to help communicate and give balance.

PRINCIPLES ON THE LANGUAGE OF LOVE

Gary Chapman wrote the book, *The 5 Love Languages.* In the book, he describes the five love languages as 1. Quality Time, 2. Words of Affirmation, 3. Gifts, 4. Acts of Service 5. Physical Touch.

- Quality time- focused and undivided attention spent together.

- Words of Affirmation – verbal complements that express your love and appreciation.

- Gifts- tangible symbols that reflect your thoughtfulness and effort.

- Acts of Service- any act that eases the burden of responsibilities.

- Physical touch- a non-sexual that reinforces your presence.

My love languages are quality time and acts of service. I love taking care of my family. Oddly, cleaning up after them and cooking meals gives me joy. I know I am doing something that they need. Yes, it gets overwhelming at times, but I'm still grateful to be able to do it.

My husband and I spend quality time when we lay in bed talking and watching movies together or going on a date. Luke's love language consisted of giving gifts and quality time. Every so often, I would buy him something special unexpectedly just to let him know I was thinking of him, and that he was appreciated. It can be something has small as buying his favorite food, candy, or something as big and fancy as a watch or an expensive shirt.

Part Two

Building A Lasting Marriage

Section IV

THE INGREDIENTS OF MARRIAGE

Chapter Eleven

Love, Honor and Respect

In this section we will discuss things I have learned to implement in marriage. I want to begin with honor. **Honor** refers to holding your spouse in the highest regard, both in person and away from them. This means speaking kindly of them when among family and friends; not saying things that will damage their character or alter other people's opinion of them. To honor could also mean conducting yourself in a manner that is pleasing to your spouse. No husband wants to hear that their wife is extra flirtatious or un-lady like when her husband is not around. A wife doesn't want to hear that their husband is in public drinking and using obscenities or entertaining multiple women on the side. You want to do things that your spouse would be proud to be associated with you. Remember you are a representation of your spouse. Whatever you do not only

70

affects you, but your spouse as well. You never want to do anything that will cause hurt or shame to fall upon your spouse. "What's done in the dark will come to the light."

Respect is like honor but instead focuses more on the feelings and emotions that you have of yourself and others. Before you can have respect for others, you must respect yourself. Respect for yourself involves your morals, standards, and boundaries. It refers to how you treat yourself. Since I have respect for myself, I don't allow others to talk down, belittle, degrade me, or cause physical harm to me. I don't do things to draw attention to myself like dress provocatively or flaunt my body. I set boundaries and have high expectations. In return, I treat my spouse and others in the same way. I wouldn't do anything to someone that I wouldn't want done to me. We must remember what love is according to the bible.

Love is powerful! Love is beautiful! When you love someone, you will know. You will think about them all the time and want to spend time with them. When you love someone, you want the best for them. You want to see them happy. You will go out of your way to do kind things for them. Love can be expressed in various forms. It can be shown verbally by saying I love you, and it can be shown physically by giving hugs, kisses, massages, soft touches or simply a soft brush. Love can be expressed through writing notes, letters and/or purchasing cards. Love can be expressed through the purchase of gifts both big and small. It can also be shown through spending quality time together.

Love is patient and understanding. Yes, there may be times when you are not on the same page, and you may not be getting along, but despite those things, you will still love and care for one another. You are still concerned about their well-being. Love doesn't disappear simply because you are mad. Having love for one another will allow you to take a step back, breathe and re-group. You will be able to come back to the situation calmer and hopefully more levelheaded. You will be open to finding a resolution. Love shouldn't be conditional. Love shouldn't be based on appearances, finances, or your status.

When you love someone, you are thoughtful and considerate. You care about the other person's feelings, interests, and their concerns. You want to make sure they are doing okay. You check in with them and ask, "How are you doing?" How are you feeling? "Is there anything I can do to help?" You are willing to compromise and do things that the other person likes. You are flexible and open. Love is reciprocal. It is a give and take. One person shouldn't be putting in all the work and effort.

Love is forgiving. Love is knowing that we are all human and we are all capable of making mistakes. We don't know everything. We are not perfect. We are going to mess up and get things wrong sometimes. We may not say something correctly or act as we should. Love is being able to admit when you have done wrong and make steps to make amends. It is making accountability for your actions; not playing the blame game. When you can forgive, you make room to heal. 1 Corinthians 13:4-8 states

4 Love is patient, love is kind. It does not envy, it does not boast, it is not proud. 5 It does not dishonor others, it is not self-seeking, it is not easily angered, it keeps no record of

wrongs.6 Love does not delight in evil but rejoices with the truth. 7 It always protects, always trusts, always trusts, always hopes, always perseveres. 8 Love never fails. But where there are prophecies, they will cease; where there are tongues, they will be stilled; where there is knowledge, it will pass away.

Sacrifice There will be times when you will have to put the wants and needs of your family above yourself. You may be dead tired and have no energy but, meals will have to be cooked, clothes will need to be washed and sex with your spouse will be a must. You must reach down into yourself and find the energy to press through.

Marriage won't always be 100/100, sometimes if we can be honest it will be 70/70, 70/40 or 80/20. It may even be 100 one way depending on the situation however it should always strive to be 100/100 of two people giving their all for the marriage. Regardless of what the ratio may be, you have to remember why you are doing what you are doing. You made a commitment to care for your spouse and family; to be their partner. Sometimes in a partnership you may be required to take on more of the slack. This may be in finances, household chores or caring for kids and loved ones. Your efforts may sometimes go unnoticed, and you won't always feel supported or appreciated, but know that it matters, and it is needed. God has placed you in this person's life for a reason. He is entrusting you to take care of them. Do what is needed and what is right, and God will honor your efforts. Do your work unto the Lord, not unto man.

As a wife and mother, I am constantly making sacrifices for the sake of my family. I have turned down jobs and opportunities because they didn't align with the needs of my family. I have passed on higher paying salaries simply because they either had travel requirements or long hours. My current position doesn't pay as much as I would like, but it offers me benefits and flexibility. My children are young. They are now at the age where they can participate in sports and school activities, because of my hours, I am able to take them to practices and attend their games. I am off in the evenings, so I can prepare a hot meal for my husband and make sure the home is tidy when he gets off work. That is more important to me right now than making money through working long hours. Maybe when they are older, they will require less time and attention, and then I can revisit some of my goals and dreams.

As women, we are often taught to put the needs of everyone else ahead of our own needs. We are nurturers by nature. We are caring, kind and compassionate towards the ones we love. We will move mountains and lift cars to protect them. There's nothing we wouldn't do for them. There is nothing wrong with caring for others, we just have to make sure we are also taking care of ourselves in the process. *You can't pour from an empty cup.* The same way that a car requires gas weekly, you have to refuel and re-energize yourself. Self-care is essential. Spend time alone. Enjoy your favorite hobbies and pass time. Seek out support from friends and loved ones. Pray and ask God to strengthen and restore you when you feel weak. Listen to music that will inspire you and uplift you. Read books to empower you and motivate you.

Sacrifices are okay so long as it's not the same person making all the sacrifices. When one person is expected to continuously put their goals, dreams, and aspirations on hold, this can often lead to resentment. The person that is expected to sacrifice will begin to feel like their needs are not being met or they are not being cared for. It's vital that each person be willing to make sacrifices.

There was a period during my marriage where my husband was changing jobs every six months. With each job, there would be a reason or excuse as to why he left that job. I couldn't understand his reasons for the life of me. I felt that he wasn't thinking of me or the kids. I felt as if he was only thinking about the financial impact it would have on our household. He didn't think about the stress or emotional toil that he was making for us. He just knew that he wanted to do something different, so he did it. This brought out a lot of anger and frustration within me. I felt like he was dumping all the responsibilities on me. I felt like he was free to change jobs at the drop of a dime, because he knew he had me to fall back upon. He knew I was secure in my position, and that I had desires to change jobs, but I didn't because of my responsibilities.

I told him how it made me feel. I let him know that I didn't feel protected or secure. I didn't feel like I could depend on him, and I really needed his support. When I presented it to him that way, he understood how I felt and the job hopping eventually stopped. Thank you, Jesus! Sacrifices don't have to be hard. Communication is key. There is a possibility that you may be able to do the things that you seek out to do, along as both people are on board. Again, you may not get everything that you want, but you may be able to get some. Together, you can come up with a plan that works for everyone involved.

Chapter Twelve

Compromise

Marriage is about give and take. No one person gets to have everything their way. The key is to be able to come together and make decisions that serve the union mutually. This could be on something as big as where to live, what cars to buy or what school to put the kids in, or something as small as which movie to watch, what's for dinner or who gets the remote?

There will be times when you won't be able to agree. This is when you will decide to meet in the middle. Maybe your spouse gets to pick the movie, but you get to pick the snacks. Maybe you watch something they want to watch this time, and you pick next time. The point is to make sure each partner has a voice and input into the decision-making process. No one wants to be treated like a child and told what to do. No one wants to have their input ignored or disregarded. Marriage is a partnership, not a dictatorship. Marriage should be about teamwork; coming together to solve a problem. Being able to come together to create a solution builds a close bond. Not to mention, it can be fun.

When my husband and I were looking for our second home, we had different ideas of what it would look like. He wanted something big and elaborate; 4 bedrooms, 2+ bathrooms, 2 living rooms, 2 dining rooms, a pool, and a huge backyard. I wanted something more traditional, affordable, and easier to maintain since I did the majority of the cleaning. We looked at several houses before settling on one that met both of our needs. We got the bedrooms and bathrooms but an open floor plan that allows the living room to open into the dining room which was great for entertaining because you could see everyone, and everyone felt included. We didn't get the pool but that was fine because neither one of us knew how to maintain a pool. We opted for a smaller back yard when I mentioned having to cut more grass and the fact that the kids never go outside. In the end, it all worked out.

Just because you decided to get married that does not mean that either of you must give up your personal style and interest. The goal is to find a way to bring everything together in a way that works for the relationship.

Faith

No marriage can stand without faith. Regardless of what your religious preference is, you must have faith. I am a Christian. I believe in God and Jesus Christ. He is the father of all. Without him, I would be nothing. I know that he is real because I have seen him come through for me, time and time again. There were times when I didn't think I was going to make it and he stepped in. God is my healer, provider, protector, and anchor. He gives me peace and restores my soul. I am grateful that I can depend on him. I talk to him through my prayers. When I'm stressed, uncertain or in doubt, he is always there guiding me and directing my steps. I trust him. I know that he will be there for me. He has never let me down. I turn to him to help me in my marriage, on my job and with my family.

I'm thankful that I can cry out to him, and he never ignores me. He always has a listening ear for me. He is never too busy. Whenever I need encouragement, I can count on his word in the Bible. There is literally a scripture in the Bible for any trials that you may face. In the Bible it says, nothing is new under the sun. That means whatever you are going through, someone else has already gone through it and the Bible gives advice on how to handle it. Whenever I need a pick-me-up, I sing his praises. Gospel music calms me and settles my anxiety. The lyrics to the songs inspire me. I'm thankful that he places people in my life that love me enough to pray over me and for me.

My marriage is stronger today because of God. People prayed on our behalf, they also stepped in, counseled, and advised us. They are not just ordinary people, but God fearing, faith-based believers who live to please God. They uphold his word and his commandments. They live out God's way in their everyday actions. Yes, we are all human and we may sin from time to time, but God is there to forgive us.

My relationship with God has gotten stronger as I have become an adult and that is because I have seen firsthand what he can do. I've seen him increase my finances, restore my health, protect my children and family, and regulate my mind. I'm thankful that I have a spouse that was born and raised in the church and has his own personal relationship with God. I've seen him pray over me and our children; because of his relationship with God, I trust him to lead me. I'm willing to follow him, as he follows Christ. I've seen God mend broken relationships in my family and resolve conflict in my home. God has given me a vision, to share my stories and provide insight to others to help them the same way HE has helped me. I know HE has more in store for me. HE is going to help me live out my vision and reap all the benefits and rewards to bless my children and their future children.

Chapter Thirteen

Trust

Trust is a feeling that is created after being with someone for a period of time. It comes from being open and honest with them. It means that you can be vulnerable around this person. When you trust someone, you are free to be yourself. You don't feel judged or criticized. You feel understood and accepted, regardless of your flaws or faults. You usually build trust after spending time with a person. You get to see them in their element.

You see how they react around friends/family. *Are they consistent? Do they remain the same regardless of who is around? Do they hold true to their morals, values and standards or are they easily persuaded?* You can usually tell how trustworthy a person is by their level of loyalty. Do they keep other people's secrets or are they a gossip? Do they keep their word? Do they do what they say they are going to do, when they say they are going to do it?

Trust takes time to build but *can be broken in seconds*. Once trust has been broken, it may be hard to repair. Sometimes, the ability to be able to trust a person has a lot to do with your past. If a person misused your trust, when a similar offense occurs, it may trigger something deep within you. It's important to allow time to heal from past traumas so you don't project that into your current relationship. If you came out of a relationship were someone was constantly lying or cheating, you may be tempted to look for those actions in your current situation. Now you start second guessing everything they say. You may be tempted to check their phone, go through their emails, or follow them around to check their whereabouts. All of these actions are unhealthy and a sign of your lack of trust.

If you don't trust them, you shouldn't be with them! If your spouse is doing something that is triggering negative emotions in you, be honest and upfront about your feelings. Let them know you have concerns. If there is nothing to be worried about, it should be no problem for them to reassure you. If they get defensive, that may be cause for concern. Just make sure that you are not falsely accusing them of things. Don't create problems that are not there. Don't project your fears and insecurities onto your partner. This could potentially sabotage the relationship and you don't want that. You don't want fear to mess up a good thing.

Chapter Fourteen

Communication

Communication is a big part of marriage. Being able to express your feelings, concerns, ideas, and passions are important. You want to create a space that your partner feels comfortable enough to approach you and be vulnerable. You want to be open. Communication can take on various forms. You can communicate using gestures, body language and facial expressions. When communicating, it is important to consider your audience, time and tone.

Always give a person your complete eye contact when you are speaking to them and vice versa. It is a sign to them that they have your undivided attention. While they are speaking, do not be playing with your phone, watching TV or do anything distracting. Listen to them and do not respond until they finish speaking. Don't interrupt or over talk your spouse. Repeat back what you heard or ask questions if you need further clarity. Try not to make facial expressions or roll your eyes. This can be hard to do; especially if you disagree with what they are saying. This gives the impression that you are in disagreement or not listening. Don't cross your arms or turn your body away. This comes off as you are not listening or receptive to what is being communicated.

Find a communication style that works for you both.

My spouse is a texter. It helps him focus his thoughts and get everything out. We can have a disagreement at home, and he won't say a word. As soon as I get to work, I get whole paragraphs sent to me via text. Now I'm frustrated because I'm trying to work, and he is blowing up my phone. I don't care for text messages; I prefer to speak in person. It's hard to judge a person's tone and attitude through a text. So much can be misinterpreted. Yes, reading the message allows you time to take it in and think over your response, but I just don't like it. You can also write notes or letters. Watch your tone. Don't yell, talk loudly or be intimidating. This can go one of two ways. This can be perceived as a threat. It makes the receiver either shut down and withdraw from the conversation or try to match your energy and become defensive and aggressive. Now you have a shouting match.

Find the right time to have a conversation.

I hate when I'm in the middle of my favorite show and my husband walks in and starts rambling off his day. Now, I will have to pause my show and give him my undivided attention and pretend like I'm listening when I would rather be watching my show. Instead, what I would like for him to do is ask, "Is now a good time or do you think we can talk later? Don't just barge in and start talking. This gives me time to think about it and make a decision that will allow me to be fully attentive and aware. Also don't discuss issues in front of other people. It's not their business. Having a conversation about finances in front of friends while on a double date, probably isn't the ideal either. Discussing bills, or a problem with the kids at school as soon as your spouse walks through the door, isn't good timing either. My husband is not a morning person, he needs time to wake and have breakfast before he is ready to talk. I know this so I don't bombard him with information first thing in the morning.

Don't let issues build up or fester! By not addressing issues as they come along, you build bitterness and resentment. You create a long list of offenses and when the time comes to have the conversation, instead of discussing the issue at hand, now you are bringing up everything else. Communicate in a manner of respect and love. If your spouse says, hey I need a minute or can we talk about this tomorrow, respect that. Just make sure you have the conversation. Don't let them avoid it or prolong it so long, that it gets swept under the rug. Avoidance with the hopes that it will go away, doesn't help the situation.

Don't discuss disagreements in front of children. Children are innocent and should be protected. Adult matters should not include them. They should never be dragged into the argument or forced to pick sides. This is an awkward place to put a child in. You can let them know that there are healthy ways to handle disagreements. Also remember that children are sponges. They absorb everything they see and hear. Whatever you say or do could potentially be repeated to a teacher or family member. This is also how they will learn how to resolve issues.

Don't air your problems on social media. This is tacky and tasteless. No one needs to know what's going on in your home. You don't need the opinions and validation from strangers to get your point across. This just leaves a trail of mess that you will later have to clean up.

Pick your battles. One part of communication is knowing when to speak and when to be quiet. Everything that is a thought, does not need to be spoken. Some things you need to keep to yourself, especially when it is not going to help the situation. Yes, you may be right in the moment but is it important to prove it? State your position and leave it alone. You don't have to repeat yourself over and over. You learn more when you listen. If you stay quiet long enough, you will hear everything that you need to know.

"My dear brothers and sisters, take note of this: Everyone should be quick to listen, slow to speak and slow to become angry because human anger does not produce the righteousness that God desires." James 1: 19-20

Section VI

AVOIDING TRAPS WITHIN MARRIAGE

Chapter Fifteen

Feminine or Masculine Energy

When I think of the word woman, I think of soft, graceful, classy, elegant, and respectful. My mind immediately goes to shows like *Leave it to Beaver*, and *I Love Lucy*. Before Black families were represented on television, these were the images that were portrayed of how a woman should conduct herself. These women were always done up in nice outfits, beautiful hair, and make-up. They cooked meals, cared for the children, all while looking good. The home was clean and presentable. They seemed to take on a service role. They made their husbands dinner, brought him the newspaper, and catered to whatever other needs they had. I don't know if they did it out of obligation or desire, but they seemed happy to do it.

Fast forward to present day and the majority of households consist of one parent. Most women are working outside of the home, all while trying to care for children and maintain a household. Many

94

men in the Black community are incarcerated, dead, gay or father multiple children in multiple households. This has caused more women to take on a self-sufficient role, since they feel like they have to do everything themselves. They have become hard and masculine. They are becoming less reliant on men. This is causing a strain in many relationships because men feel like they have no place. They are fighting to be seen and valued in the relationship. Some women are coming off more aggressive and argumentative. They have an "I don't need you attitude or demeanor."

Reality shows and music videos have normalized women in toxic relationships being verbally and physically abused. Women are going toe to toe with men, arguing, cussing, and fighting. It is shown so much that it has become normal for young kids coming up, which is unfortunate. This is not a true representation of love and commitment. Women should not be cheated on, spoken down to, or demeaned. Women should not be subjected to disrespect regarding their bodies. Men should not be seen solely as a financial opportunity. Manhood is not established by how many children you have or women that you sleep with. There must be a level of respect and honor. A home is supposed to be a place of peace, not constant chaos, and frustration.

I am a victim of operating in masculine energy. I've always been self-sufficient. I've been on my own since I graduated from high school. I always felt like I had no one I could turn to or depend on, so I learned how to get things on my own. This made it hard for me in relationships. There wasn't room for a man to take care of me or do nice things for me because I wasn't used to it. I didn't know how to accept gifts, help or compliments. I often turned down help because I didn't want to feel like I owed someone anything. I always thought he had a hidden agenda. I thought if a man did something for me, he must want something in return. I had to learn that it is okay to allow someone to come in and help me from time to time. It's okay to allow someone to open the door for me, carry my groceries or pay for my dinner. It's okay for a man to compliment me and me say thank you without it meaning something else. It's okay to receive nice gifts. I deserve all these things and I can do all these things for my mate because he deserves it too.

Chapter Sixteen

Divorce

I won't go into great detail about divorce because the goal is to stay together. Yes, divorce happens; more often than not, but that's because people are giving up too easily, comparing their lives to others or committing adultery. Betraying your spouse can lead to an outcome that leaves both husband and wife feeling alone. The first problem that can lead to divorce if unattended is comparison.

Comparison

"Comparison is the theft of joy." Comparison is like envy-- wanting what someone else has. It will cause you to take your attention and focus off your own life and situation and epitomize other people's lives. It takes you from a place of gratitude and appreciation to one of jealousy and envy. When you are married, comparison opens a

box of confusion. It plants seeds of destruction. You start to second guess yourself. You begin to feel like you should have what the other person has or be further along in life. But I'm here to tell you, there will always be someone who is more successful, prettier, has more money, or a nicer car. None of those things matter. All of that is temporary.

Eventually, that will get old. What matters is the core of a person. How do they treat you? Where you are in life and everything that you have, is something that you prayed for and worked hard to accomplish. When you focus on these things, you find yourself in a place of happiness and joy. You feel fulfilled. It's when you take your focus off these things and start to look at other people's lives that you begin to feel stressed, depressed, and anxious, hence the phrase, "theft of joy". You desired the house, car, career, spouse, and family that you currently have, so why does it feel like it's not enough?

In the age of social media, people are constantly posting pictures of a happier time. It could be a vacation trip, an outing with friends/family, dinner at a nice restaurant or a concert, but these are all snippets of the person's life. It doesn't show their day-to-day life. It doesn't capture the moments when they are sad, lonely, depressed, hurt or simply having a bad day. Nobody wants to see that. Those moments don't get many likes, but they happen and are real. Everyone has moments that are not so popular or glamorous. We are all human and we all have struggles. Before you envy a person and wish you had their body, money, and success- man or woman, ask yourself how much of that is real?

Most of the bodies that you see today have been surgically enhanced, or they have a personal chef or trainer that can help achieve the look they desire. The average person cannot accomplish this on their own. When it comes to wanting what someone else has or someone's money, just know that some people are living beyond their means, which is why they have nice clothes, shoes and purses and can take luxury trips. They may have maxed out their credit cards, extended themselves in personal loans, or they could be living off someone else. You never know what's behind a person's story. One leading cause of divorce as we mentioned earlier is infidelity.

Infidelity

Infidelity is one of the top causes of divorce. When you get married you don't go into the marriage thinking that your spouse is going to cheat on you, but unfortunately, sometimes it happens. The reasons may vary; lack of sex, lack of emotional connection, boredom, addiction; need for variety. Whatever the reason maybe, finding yourself faced with this situation is a hard pill to swallow. What happens next can go one or two ways. You can deal with it; have a conversation to find out what led to this; forgive, seek counsel and try to move passed it. Just know if you choose to forgive, trust must be restored, but it's up to your partner to help you restore your trust.

The other option is to end the marriage. Cheating is a deal breaker to some. The number of times and the number of people can play a huge role in determining whether to stay or leave. If your spouse cheated one time, admitted it, expressed regret, and remorse, then you may be able to forgive that offense. But if your spouse is just out there, wilding out, sleeping with multiple people, well that's a wrap. The marriage has been defiled not just one time, but multiple times. They made a conscious decision, repeatedly, with no regards for your feelings or well-being. That is just outright disrespect. If you decide to stay in that type of scenario, well you are sending a signal that you are accepting your spouse's behavior and you may as well expect the behavior to continue.

You may find that there are many opportunities to cheat, but you must have self-discipline. You must know there is more at risk. This one act can ruin your family and your reputation. The best thing you can do is to avoid any type of situation that tempts you to cheat. Don't surround yourself with people that do not support your marriage and tempt you to do things that will jeopardize your marriage. Don't watch certain movies, shows, or look at certain photos. Don't listen to certain types of music. Don't download certain apps to your phone if you know it can lead to potential problems for you. Don't stay in contact with exes. Don't befriend the opposite sex if it's going to create future problems.

If you are the victim of infidelity, know that it is not your fault. Cheating is a selfish act. It has more to do with the person committing the act than the person on the receiving end. Even if they say, "you weren't available, you didn't give me enough sex, your work is more important than me or you care more about the kids than me," it's not your fault. Those are all excuses for them to do what they want. Those things can be worked on.

When Divorce Arises

When divorce arises in marriage it's because both have forgotten the purpose of marriage. Divorce can be catastrophic. It doesn't just affect the two people involved but it also affects your children, family, and friends. It is awkward and uncomfortable, and not to mention costly. It is also time-consuming. Some divorces can be quick, and others can take years. It depends on the amount of assets that must be divided, and the wants of the people involved. Pettiness can make it turn nasty. Every reader needs to know that divorce is preventable. True commitment in marriage takes hard work and effort. If you do the things outlined in the previous chapters, you can reduce your chances of divorce. The main thing for both you and your spouse to decide is that divorce can't be an option within your marriage. Even the very idea of divorce must be removed from the table. If you eliminate the possibility of divorce, it will force you to work together to produce manageable solutions. You can stay together and be miserable, or you can find resources and outcomes to make the situation better.

My advice is to avoid divorce if it is at all possible. Communicate regularly. Seek counsel. Pray. Work hard to reconcile and come to an agreement that works for everyone. Unfortunately, my marriage to Luke didn't last long. We divorced after three years of marriage at his request. I was devastated and caught off guard nonetheless, the experiences and the lessons I learned prepared me for my next and current marriage. They helped me to become the mother and wife that I am today. I have more patience and understanding. I show more love and compassion. I am better equipped to handle problems and situations that come my way. I am fortunate to have experienced love not one time but two. I know what it feels like to have love, lose it and then find it again. I have a greater appreciation for our union and our family. I treasure the moments that we spent together and the memories that we create. I am now married to Darrell Shiner and we have been together for about ten years now. We share a son together and I am a stepmother to his son.

Conclusion

Thank you for taking the time to read this book. I hope you read something that will transform the way you think about marriage. Marriage is a beautiful thing! It can be fun, joyous, and exhilarating. Having someone to share your life with can be amazing. Having the ability to have a life partner that you can spend time with laughing and creating memories with is remarkable.

Marriage can also be hard. There will be good days and there will be bad days. There will be times when you want to give up and throw in the towel. If anybody tells you different, they aren't being honest. It will require hard work between you and your spouse to make it last. There will be challenges that will test your faith, resilience, and patience. Challenges may appear in the areas of communication, finances, child rearing, and health, there is no avoiding this. The key is to wake up every morning and make a choice, choose your marriage, choose your spouse, choose love.

Thank you and be blessed!

I'm Married Now What

I'm Married Now What

I'm Married Now What

I'm Married Now What

I'm Married Now What

I'm Married Now What

I'm Married Now What

I'm Married Now What

I'm Married Now What

I'm Married Now What

I'm Married Now What

I'm Married Now What

I'm Married Now What

I'm Married Now What

I'm Married Now What

I'm Married Now What

I'm Married Now What

I'm Married Now What

I'm Married Now What

I'm Married Now What

I'm Married Now What

I'm Married Now What

I'm Married Now What

I'm Married Now What

I'm Married Now What

I'm Married Now What

I'm Married Now What

I'm Married Now What

I'm Married Now What

I'm Married Now What

I'm Married Now What

I'm Married Now What

I'm Married Now What

I'm Married Now What

I'm Married Now What

I'm Married Now What

I'm Married Now What

I'm Married Now What

I'm Married Now What

I'm Married Now What

I'm Married Now What

I'm Married Now What

I'm Married Now What

CPSIA information can be obtained
at www.ICGtesting.com
Printed in the USA
JSHW040458120523
41609JS00006B/164